Dirty Jobs

Garbage Collector

Jack Zayarny

MEDIA ENHANCED BOOKS
AV2 BY WEIGL
ADDED VALUE • AUDIO VISUAL
www.av2books.com

Published by AV² by Weigl
350 5th Avenue, 59th Floor
New York, NY 10118

Websites: www.av2books.com www.weigl.com

Library of Congress Control Number: 2014934639

ISBN 978-1-4896-0998-4 (hardcover)
ISBN 978-1-4896-0999-1 (softcover)
ISBN 978-1-4896-1000-3 (single-user eBook)
ISBN 978-1-4896-1001-0 (multi-user eBook)

Printed in the United States of America in North Mankato, Minnesota
1 2 3 4 5 6 7 8 9 0 18 17 16 15 14

042014
WEP150314

Senior Editor: Aaron Carr
Designer: Mandy Christiansen

Every reasonable effort has been made to trace ownership and to obtain permission to reprint copyright material. The publishers would be pleased to have any errors or omissions brought to their attention so that they may be corrected in subsequent printings.

Weigl acknowledges Getty Images as its primary image supplier for this title.

Contents

What Is a Garbage Collector?

Garbage collectors are workers that help gather waste from homes and businesses. Many tons (metric tons) of waste need to be picked up and moved every day. Garbage collectors are responsible for this task. It is also their job to dispose of this waste correctly by taking it to **landfills** or other sites, such as **recycling plants**. Most towns and cities have a garbage collection service.

Every day, the United States makes about 1.35 billion pounds (612 million kilograms) of waste. This means that Americans throw away the weight of 6,750 blue whales every day. Since this is a very large amount, garbage collection is an important part of a properly working society.

Many Names, One Job

Garbage collectors are known by many names. They are sometimes called waste management employees, sanitation engineers, or simply garbage collectors. Many garbage collectors own their own businesses. Others work with **municipal** governments or large waste management companies.

In 2008, 31 percent of municipal waste was made up of paper products.

Where They Work

Garbage collectors work in many settings. This ranges from neighborhood streets where the garbage is picked up to the landfills where it is buried. Most of their work takes place outside. They often work in difficult weather conditions, including rain and snow.

There are more than 135,000 garbage trucks on the road in the United States.

Right on Time

Houses, apartment and office buildings, factories, and parks are all places that garbage collectors will visit during their work day. In residential areas, waste management employees may visit up to 300 homes in a single 8-hour shift. Garbage collectors typically work on a single route.

Businesses often have agreements with waste management companies. These agreements set out rules about when and how often garbage collectors will pick up waste.

Some household garbage bins weigh more than 100 pounds (45 kilograms) when they are full.

A Dirty Job

Collecting garbage is a dirty job. Much of the waste people throw away is unclean and harmful to touch or smell. Garbage collectors often pick up and carry dirty waste bins to their trucks. They have to spend large amounts of time in waste storage areas. Even if the waste bins are picked up by a machine, garbage workers are still exposed to the smell and are expected to pick up any leftover trash.

Waste Collection Dangers

More than 12 percent of America's solid waste is made up of food products. By the time garbage workers come in contact with these products, the products are rotting and giving off a foul smell. There can be a risk of disease when touching or smelling chemicals or products that have been left to rot for too long.

The average American produces 4.6 pounds (2 kilograms) of waste every day.

Garbage collectors often have to handle items such as used diapers, dirty towels, containers of dirt or dust, and paint. These materials are often mixed together, and garbage collectors have to handle these items many times during their workday.

Raccoons are able to open most lids and latches using their front paws.

In 2008, only 23 percent of glass that was thrown away was recycled.

Recycling

Recycling is the practice of changing waste into usable material. Cans and bottles are often reused to create similar products. Metals and plastics can be melted down and used as materials in a range of industries. Food and other **biodegradable** items create **compost** as they decay. This compost is rich in **nutrients** and can be used as **fertilizer** on farms.

35 percent
of all waste in the United States can be recycled.

Recycling one aluminum can saves enough energy to run a television for three hours.

More than
100,000 cans
are recycled every minute in the United States.

250,000,000 trees could be saved every year if all newspapers were recycled.

All in a Day's Work

A typical day in the life of a garbage collector begins early in the morning. Many routes may start as early as 4 a.m. Garbage collectors often work in pairs. One worker drives the garbage truck and operates the lift to pick up large bins. The other worker helps move the bins into position and empties smaller containers. This is called a dump cycle. After the route is finished, the garbage collectors drive the waste to a **processing plant**, where biodegradable and recyclable waste is separated from other garbage.

"Being a garbage collector can be a great job," says José, a sanitation worker from Minneapolis, Minnesota. "I work for a large waste management company that services around 50,000 houses in the city. The job is demanding and the hours can be difficult, but it has some good benefits as well. I never liked working in an office, and being a garbage collector gives me a chance to work outside. It also keeps me in great physical shape, and the job never gets boring. I enjoy being able to help the community."

Though they may ride on a garbage truck, garbage collectors walk an average of 20 miles (32 kilometers) a day on the job.

Waste Collection and Disposal Cycle

Garbage collection is just the first step in the waste management process. Once the waste is collected, it is taken to a processing plant. There, it can be organized and moved to either a recycling plant or a landfill. Even then the process is not complete. Some power stations create electricity by burning garbage. Recyclable materials are remade into new products that are sold and end up in people's homes once again.

Staying Safe

Garbage collectors face many hazards while they work. They sometimes handle medical waste, such as syringes, and dangerous chemicals. Rotting garbage can also carry diseases and may be home to pests and other dangerous animals. To stay safe on the job, garbage collectors must wear the proper safety equipment.

Safety Vest

Garbage collectors wear safety vests to make them more visible to other people. These vests are bright orange. Most vests have reflective patches, which catch the light and make their wearers more visible at night.

Work Boots

Work boots allow the garbage collector to walk in dirty or slippery areas. Wide soles and rubber grips provide a stable, solid platform when carrying heavy weights such as trash cans. Boots can also have steel toes to protect feet from falling objects.

Safety First

By law, garbage collectors must wear safety equipment at all times. Many companies provide equipment and uniforms for their workers. Others require garbage collectors to buy their own safety equipment. Different types of safety equipment may be required, depending on the laws in each area.

Hard Hat

Protecting the head from falling objects is very important for garbage collectors. They often work in areas where trash is piled high and may fall. Hard hats are made from strong plastic and have cushions inside to help absorb impact.

Gloves, Masks, and Earphones

Gloves protect the garbage worker's skin from touching harmful materials such as chemicals. Masks are used in areas where the smell is too strong or when dealing with poisonous fumes. Earphones help protect hearing in areas where machinery is loud.

Tools of the Trade

The most important tool that garbage collectors have is the garbage truck. The garbage truck is a dump truck that has been modified for storing and moving waste. The garbage is stored in a large metal bin on the back of the truck. Most trucks have a moving wall inside of the box that presses the trash into smaller pieces. This allows garbage trucks to store more waste during a single trip.

Types of Trucks

The three most common types of garbage trucks are front loaders, rear loaders, and side loaders.

Front Loaders

Front loaders are the most common type of garbage truck. Two **arm forks** on the front pick up and empty garbage bins into the box on the back of the truck.

Rear Loaders

Rear loaders have an opening in the rear where garbage collectors can throw bags of trash.

Side Loaders

Side loaders tip their containers to the side. They can either be loaded by hand or with the help of a mechanical arm.

Then

In the past, garbage collection was done by hand. Garbage collectors went from door to door and loaded garbage in the back of a carriage or truck. At the landfill, garbage was also emptied by hand.

Now

Garbage collectors use large dump trucks that do much of the heavy lifting for them. This is a much faster process. At the processing plant, trucks automatically dump waste into containers for sorting.

The Garbage Collector's Role

Garbage collection is a key part of the smooth operation of a city or town. Waste has to be removed quickly, or it can create pollution and spread disease. The garbage collector serves an important role in this process. Most waste in residential areas is collected using **curbside pick up**. People are usually given separate bins for garbage, organic waste such as food, and recyclable materials such as plastic. Every week, the full bins are placed at the curb, where they are emptied by garbage collectors.

"It's a dirty job, but someone has to do it."

Processing Waste

Organic waste such as food often goes through processing plants to landfills, where it is stored and given time to decompose. Most landfills are located in areas far away from where people live. Landfills are also placed far from water sources to avoid polluting the water. About 15 percent of the waste is burned in **incinerators**. The energy created from this can be used to provide power to homes and factories.

Americans throw away enough garbage every day to fill 63,000 garbage trucks.

Recycling

Recycling is an important part of properly dealing with waste. Plastic, glass, paper, and even oil and steel can all be recycled to save money and energy. Recycling also helps protect the environment.

61 billion aluminum cans were recycled in the U.S. in 2011.

1 million tons (907,185 metric tons) of extra waste is produced in the United States between Thanksgiving and Christmas.

Less than 1 percent of plastic bags are recycled.

Becoming a Garbage Collector

The right skills and attitude are needed in order to become a garbage collector. The job requires lifting heavy objects, dealing with dirt and odors, and working at any hour in any weather. A high school diploma is often needed to become a garbage collector. It is also important to be in good physical shape. Most training is done on the job.

Salaries for workers in the waste removal and waste management industry vary in different areas. As a rule, garbage collectors earn more in large cities, as there is more waste and larger areas to cover. The chart below shows the average annual salary for different positions within the waste management industry.

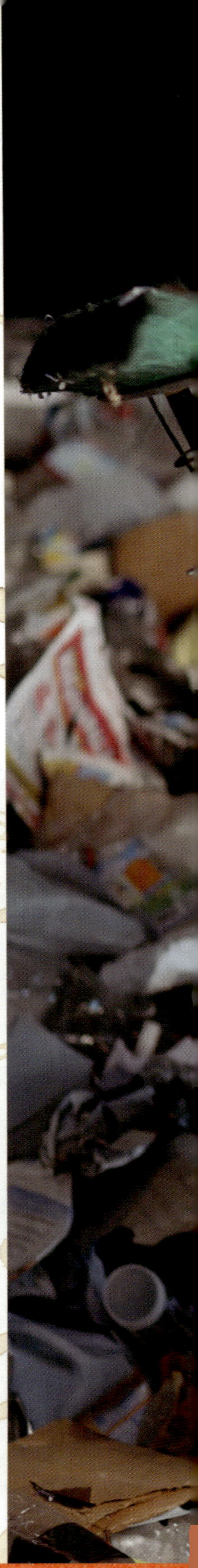

Average Salary per Year

Customer Service	$27,500
Accountant	$40,500
Garbage Truck Driver	$41,400
Route Manager	$60,200
Operations Manager	$63,625
Plant Manager	$72,250
Project Manager	$77,173

Packaging materials make up one-third of the garbage found in the average landfill.

Is This Career for You?

A career as a garbage collector is not easy, but it means filling an important role in the everyday lives of the people around you. It can be rewarding work that helps protect the environment and gives back to the community.

✓ Training

Garbage collectors are usually trained by their more experienced coworkers. This training includes learning proper garbage handling rules and how to operate a garbage truck.

✓ Education

A high school diploma is usually required to work as a garbage collector. A valid driver's license is needed to be able to drive garbage trucks.

✓ Application

To apply, waste removal companies can be contacted directly. Many are part of the town or city government and can be applied to by contacting the municipal government. Others advertise on the internet and job boards.

Career Connections

Plan your garbage collection career with this activity. Follow the instructions outlined in the steps below to complete the process of becoming a garbage collector.

1. Speak to your neighborhood garbage collector. This person can answer your questions and give you an inside look into the position.

2. Visit a job fair or a university career center to find out more information about working in the waste management industry.

3. Work on your resumé. A good resumé that shows your strongest skills can go a long way toward attracting the attention of potential employers.

4. Call or write to a waste management company. Say that you are interested in a garbage collector position and ask for advice on how to apply.

1. Decide if you have the personality and attitude for collecting garbage. If you do not mind a dirty job, can work flexible hours, and are in good physical shape, this may be the job for you.
2. Consider the skills you will need to have. Having a valid driver's license or a certificate to operate machines such as a forklift will be a bonus.
3. Contact employers for requirements. Look for private and public waste removal companies. Get in touch with them and find out what they are looking for from potential applicants.
4. Apply for the position and arrange an interview. If successful, come to the interview with knowledge of the industry and your skills.

Quiz

1. How much waste is produced in the United States each day?

2. How many homes do garbage collectors typically visit in one shift?

3. In which cities were the first aluminum recycling plants built in the United States?

4. How much of America's solid waste is food products?

5. Where do garbage collectors drive the waste after completing their shift?

6. What are the three most common types of garbage trucks?

7. Name three pieces of equipment a garbage collector must have.

8. Do garbage collectors need formal education?

9. What percentage of garbage is burned in incinerators?

10. Where can more information about working as a garbage collector be found?

Answers: 1. 1.35 billion pounds (612 million kg) 2. Up to 300 3. Chicago and Cleveland 4. More than 12 percent 5. A processing plant 6. Front loaders, side loaders, and rear loaders 7. Vest, boots, hard hat/earphones/gloves/mask 8. They need a high school diploma 9. 15 percent 10. At a career fair, job center, or on the internet

Key Words

arm forks: metal bars on the front of a garbage truck used to lift dumpster bins

biodegradable: able to be broken down into organic parts

compost: material made after organic items decay and break down

curbside pick up: process where garbage collectors pick up waste from the curb in residential neighborhoods

fertilizer: substance containing nutrients used to help plants and crops grow

incinerators: machines that use heat to break down waste

landfills: isolated areas where garbage is stored long-term

municipal: something that relates to a town or city, such as its local government

nutrients: things that help plants and organisms grow

processing plant: a location where collected waste is organized and separated

recycling plants: places where materials such as plastic and cardboard are processed to be reused later

Index

Log on to www.av2books.com

AV² by Weigl brings you media enhanced books that support active learning. Go to www.av2books.com, and enter the special code found on page 2 of this book. You will gain access to enriched and enhanced content that supplements and complements this book. Content includes video, audio, weblinks, quizzes, a slide show, and activities.

AV² Online Navigation

Audio
Listen to sections of the book read aloud.

Book Pages
AV² pages directly correspond to pages in the book.

Video
Watch informative video clips.

Embedded Weblinks
Gain additional information for research.

Key Words
Study vocabulary, and complete a matching word activity.

Try This!
Complete activities and hands-on experiments.

Quizzes
Test your knowledge.

Slide Show
View images and captions, and prepare a presentation.

AV² was built to bridge the gap between print and digital. We encourage you to tell us what you like and what you want to see in the future.

Sign up to be an AV² Ambassador at www.av2books.com/ambassador.

Due to the dynamic nature of the Internet, some of the URLs and activities provided as part of AV² by Weigl may have changed or ceased to exist. AV² by Weigl accepts no responsibility for any such changes. All media enhanced books are regularly monitored to update addresses and sites in a timely manner. Contact AV² by Weigl at 1-866-649-3445 or av2books@weigl.com with any questions, comments, or feedback.